LOOKING AT LABELS:

THE INSIDE STORY

ALL NATURAL

Benito's

BURRITOS

HIGH
IN FIBER!

Benito's
BURRITOS

Slim Goodbody's
LIGHTEN UP
SERIES

Crabtree Publishing Company
www.crabtreebooks.com

Series Development and Packaging: John Burstein, Slim Goodbody Corp.
Senior Script Development: Phoebe Backler
Managing Editor: Valerie J. Weber
Designer and Illustrator: Ben McGinnis
Graphic Design Agency: Adventure Advertising
Instructional Designer: Alan Backler, Ph. D.
Content Consultant: Betty Hubbard, Ed. D., Certified Health Education Specialist
Project Editor: Reagan Miller

Library and Archives Canada Cataloguing in Publication

Burstein, John.
    Looking at labels : the inside story / Slim Goodbody.

(Slim Goodbody's lighten up!)
ISBN 978-0-7787-3917-3 (bound).--ISBN 978-0-7787-3935-7 (pbk.)

      1. Nutrition--Juvenile literature. 2. Food--Labeling--Juvenile
literature. 3. Food--Composition--Juvenile literature. I. Title. II. Series:
Goodbody, Slim. Slim Goodbody's lighten up!
TX551.G66 2008   j613.2
C2008-900728-X

Library of Congress Cataloging-in-Publication Data

Burstein, John.
    Looking at labels : the inside story / John Burstein.
      p. cm. -- (Slim goodbody's lighten up!)
  Includes index.
    ISBN-13: 978-0-7787-3917-3 (rlb)
    ISBN-10: 0-7787-3917-1 (rlb)
    ISBN-13: 978-0-7787-3935-7 (pb)
    ISBN-10: 0-7787-3935-X (pb)
    1. Nutrition--Juvenile literature. 2. Food--Labeling--Juvenile literature.
3. Food--Composition--Juvenile literature. I. Title. II. Series.

  RA784.B785 2008
  613.2--dc22
                        2008003595

Crabtree Publishing Company

www.crabtreebooks.com   1-800-387-7650

Published in Canada
Crabtree Publishing
616 Welland Ave.
St. Catharines, Ontario
L2M 5V6

Published in the United States
Crabtree Publishing
PMB16A
350 Fifth Ave., Suite 3308
New York, NY 10118

Published in the United Kingdom
Crabtree Publishing
White Cross Mills
High Town, Lancaster
LA1 4XS

Published in Australia
Crabtree Publishing
386 Mt. Alexander Rd.
Ascot Vale (Melbourne)
VIC 3032

Printed in the U.S.A.

TABLE OF CONTENTS

Slim Goodbody's **LIGHTEN UP** SERIES

HELLO THERE. I'M SLIM GOODBODY,

and my greatest goal in life is to help young people across the planet become healthy and active. After all, one in three kids in the United States is overweight. Without changing their eating and exercise habits, many of these young people will become overweight adults. They risk many possible health problems like **high blood pressure** or **diabetes**.

Today, I would like to introduce you to my friend Carlos Benito. Carlos is always working on new business ideas. His newest idea is to team up with his mother to sell her delicious burritos at a local grocery store. But before they can sell their burritos, Carlos and his mother have a lot of work to do. Join Carlos as he explores the world of **nutrition** and food science!

A Brilliant Idea

Hi, my name is Carlos Benito. Ever since I was a kid, I've loved coming up with new business ideas. Over the summer, I mowed lawns and trimmed hedges all across my neighborhood. Now that school has started again, I need to come up with a new idea for a job. My goal is to save enough money to buy a dirt bike. But what could I do after school and on weekends? Let me tell you how I figured it out.

NUTRITION AND HEALTHY CHOICES

Why Eat Well?

We were talking about nutrition and making healthy choices in health class. Mr. Lawrence, our health teacher, was pacing in the front of the class. "Can any of you give me a few reasons why you should eat a healthy diet and exercise?" he asked.

I raised my hand and offered, "If you eat **nutritious** foods and exercise, it's easier to keep your body at a healthy weight. You also have less chance of getting diseases like diabetes and high blood pressure."

4

My classmate Keisha asked, "I know that fruits and vegetables are healthy. But how do you know if packaged foods like macaroni and cheese or cereal are good for you?"

"Great question, Keisha," said Mr. Lawrence. "The Nutrition Facts label on the back of the package is a very helpful tool. The information on those labels is **valid**. It was checked by food scientists that work for the federal government. You can rely on their information because they're not trying to sell you something."

"All right, but why doesn't healthy food taste as good as chips and candy bars?" asked Keisha.

I turned to her, "You need to come over to my house. My mom makes the most incredible burritos. They're healthy too!"

"It's true. His mom's burritos are out of this world!" agreed Johnny, my best friend.

"Well, why don't you bring some in for the rest of us?" asked Keisha.

AHA!

After class, my new idea hit me. "That's it! I'm going to figure out how to sell my mom's burritos at the grocery store. We could call them Benito's Burritos!" I told Johnny. "We can show people that healthy food can be delicious."

"You'll make a fortune," declared Johnny. "And maybe you'll finally be able to make enough money for your dirt bike."

SECRET RECIPES AND SERVING SIZES

The next day, I went to our local grocery store with one of my mother's freshly made bean-and-cheese burritos. Sal, the owner, was standing behind the counter.

"Hey, Sal, do you have a minute? I want to ask you something," I said.

"Sure, what's up, Carlos?" asked Sal.

"I've got a new idea for a business, and I need your help," I said. I handed him my mother's burrito.

Sal bit into the burrito. As he chewed, his eyes grew wide. "This is incredible, Carlos. Where did you get it?"

"It's my mom's secret recipe," I said grinning. "My mom and I want to start our own burrito business. We want to show people that nutritious foods can be delicious. We even have an idea for how to package the burritos, but we need a store where we can sell them."

LABEL TELLS ALL

"Wow. That's a good idea, Carlos. Well, the first thing that you need is a Nutrition Facts label," said Sal as he ate the last bite. We walked over to one of the aisles, and he pulled down a box of macaroni and cheese.

"This is the Nutrition Facts label. If you look at the top, you'll see the serving size. The serving size helps customers compare different kinds of food. As you see here, the serving size for this macaroni and cheese is 1 cup (250 ml). Serving sizes are always measured in familiar units like cups or pieces and in metric measurements like grams. Similar foods are usually measured in the same way," explained Sal.

"That makes sense," I said.

Nutrition Facts

Serving Size 1 cup (228g)
Servings Per Container 2

Amount Per Serving	
Calories 250	Calories from Fat 110

	% Daily Value*
Total Fat 12g	18%
Saturated Fat 3g	15%
Trans Fat 3g	
Cholesterol 30mg	10%
Sodium 470mg	20%
Total Carbohydrate 31g	10%
Dietary Fiber 0g	0%
Sugars 5g	
Protein 5g	

Vitamin A	4%
Vitamin C	2%
Calcium	20%
Iron	4%

*Percent Daily Values are based on a 2,000 calorie diet. Your daily values may be higher or lower depending on your calorie needs.

		2,000	2,500
	Calories		
Total Fat	Less than	65g	80g
Sat Fat	Less than	20g	25g
Cholesterol	Less than	300mg	300mg
Sodium	Less than	2,400mg	2,400mg
Total Carbohydrate		300g	375g
Dietary Fiber		25g	30g

"Once you know your serving size, you can determine the number of **calories** and all of the **nutrients** in each serving. See here," said Sal, pointing to the label, "There are 250 calories in each serving of this macaroni and cheese."

"Boy, that's tricky. There are two servings in this box. If you eat the whole thing, you are actually eating 500 calories and 24 grams of fat. I guess letting the customer know the serving size really is important," I said.

"That's right," said Sal. "And hey, when your mom's burritos are packaged up and ready for sale, come on back. Hold on to this too. It might help!" he said, tossing the box of macaroni and cheese to me.

"Great!" I said with excitement. "Thanks, Sal."

Slim Goodbody Says: Remember that the Nutrition Facts label only gives information about the food in a package. Sometimes you need to add other ingredients like oil, butter, and milk to prepare the food for eating. If you add ingredients, consider that you may also be adding fat and **sodium** as well as vitamins and minerals.

How Big Is a Benito's Burrito?

When I got home from the store, I felt swamped. I didn't realize how much work it would take to sell my mother's burritos in a store.

"How's Sal?" asked my mother when I came in the door.

"He's good," I said with a tired voice. "He told me to come back with your burritos when we package them."

"You're kidding. That's great news! Why are you so down?" she asked, looking concerned.

"We have to make our own Nutrition Facts label for your burritos. I don't have a clue how to do that," I said with a sigh.

"You know that if something is worthwhile, it takes effort, right? We can do this if we work together," said my mother. "And remember, if we do, we'll have enough money to buy you a dirt bike!"

"Good point!" I said, smiling. We sat down at the computer to get to work.

Serving Size

"The first thing we need to do is figure out our serving size," I explained, showing her Sal's box of macaroni and cheese. We went on the Internet and learned that other companies measured the serving size for their burritos in ounces (grams). Next we used my mother's small kitchen scale to weigh one of her burritos.

"One burrito is 6 ounces (170g)," I announced. "So let's say that one burrito is one serving. Next we need to figure out how many calories are in each serving."

COUNTING CALORIES

"Let's keep looking on the Web," suggested my mother. She soon found a basic website about calories. We learned the following:

- If you eat a typical 2,000-calorie diet, use this Calorie Guide to decide if a food is low or high in calories.

Calorie Guide
40 calories per serving is LOW
100 calories per serving is MODERATE
400 calories per serving is HIGH

- It is important to balance the calories that you eat with the calories that you burn through exercise and during daily activities.

- The calories that you don't burn through exercise and daily activities are stored as fat in your body.

- Compare the Nutrition Facts labels of different kinds of food products to see how many calories are in each one.

"This is interesting, but it doesn't help us figure out how to measure the number of calories in your burritos, Mom. I think we need help. I'd better ask my health teacher for advice," I said.

Slim Goodbody Says: Using the calorie guide above, decide if you think that Sal's macaroni and cheese is low, moderate, or high in calories. What if you eat the whole box? Remember, when you consume a food that is high in calories, make up for it later. Select lower-calorie foods throughout the day.

THE PERCENT DAILY VALUE

The next day, I asked Mr. Lawrence for his help creating a Nutrition Facts label. He suggested that I bring a burrito to his friend Dr. Laurie Chang, a food scientist.

"She can analyze your mother's burritos and give you all of the nutritional information that you need about them," said Mr. Lawrence.

The following week, I found Dr. Chang bent over a microscope in her lab. "Hi, my name is Carlos. Mr. Lawrence told me that you might be able to help me analyze my mother's burritos. I'm trying to make a Nutrition Facts label for them," I said.

"Of course Mr. Lawrence told me about you," she replied warmly. I handed her one of my mother's burritos. "So we will need to measure the calories and the **Percent Daily Value** of the nutrients in your mother's burrito," she explained.

"What's the Percent Daily Value?" I asked.

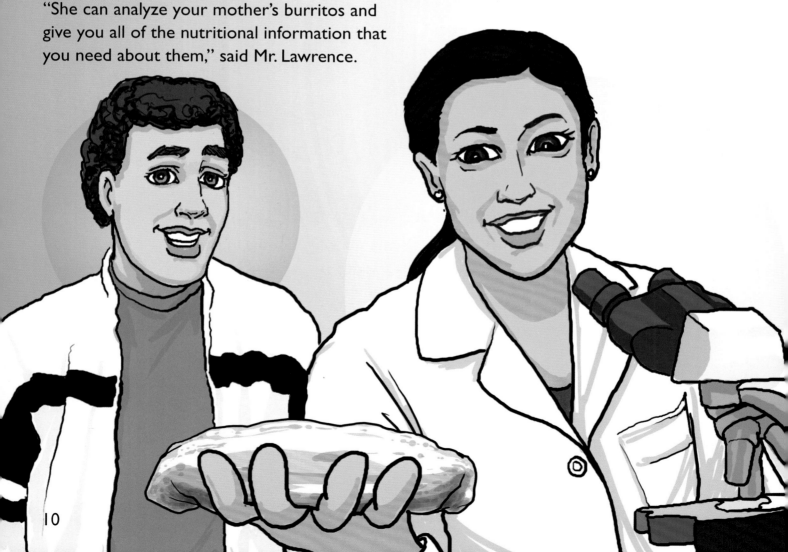

JUDGING YOUR FOOD

"It's an important part of the Nutrition Facts label. It helps **consumers** decide if the food is high or low in a nutrient. Imagine that the Nutrition Facts label on a package says that one serving of the food inside contains 20 percent of a nutrient like calcium. That means it contains 20 percent of the calcium that you need each day."

"That makes sense. And since serving sizes of similar foods are usually the same, you can compare two products to see which is more nutritious, right?" I asked.

"Correct. Now let's analyze your mom's burrito. Do you know what the serving size is?" said Laurie.

"Each burrito weighs 6 ounces (170g), so that will be our serving size," I explained.

Slim Goodbody Says: It's important to pay attention to the Percent Daily Value on the Nutrition Facts label. That way you can choose foods that are high in nutrients so that your body can grow, and you can stay healthy. You can use the Nutrition Facts label not only to help *limit* those nutrients that you want to cut back on, but also to *increase* those nutrients that you need to consume in greater amounts. Use this guide to help you decide if food is high or low in a nutrient.

Quick Guide to the Percent Daily Value (%DV)
5 percent or less
of the recommended daily value of a nutrient is **LOW**
20 percent or more
of the recommended daily value of a nutrient is **HIGH**

Now look at the Nutrition Facts label on Sal's box of macaroni and cheese on page 6. How would you rate the Percent Daily Value (%DV) for the total **carbohydrates** in one serving of the macaroni and cheese? Is it low, high, or in between?

(Answer: In between)

LIMIT THESE

Dr. Chang started analyzing the nutrients in one serving of my mother's burrito. "This is looking good so far, Carlos. Your mother's burritos have 120 calories per serving."

I thought back to the Website about calories that I found with my mother. "That means that they have a moderate number of calories. Is that bad?" I asked.

"These burritos are full of nutrients, so they are a healthy source of calories. If we were testing a sugary cereal or candy, I would feel differently. We consider the calories in sugary foods to be empty calories. Those foods don't contain many nutrients. When you eat them, you get the fattening calories without the nutrients that keep you healthy and strong," explained Dr. Chang. "Your mother's burritos are also low in sodium, **saturated fats, and trans fats**."

Calorie Guide
40 calories per serving is LOW
100 calories per serving is MODERATE
400 calories per serving is HIGH

THE DOWNSIDE OF SODIUM AND SATURATED FATS

"Sodium and saturated fats are bad for your health, right?" I asked.

"Right. Too much sodium can lead to high blood pressure. Too much saturated fat and trans fats can increase the bad **cholesterol** levels in your blood. People with high cholesterol often have problems with their hearts. They can even develop heart disease. In general, it's a good idea to avoid foods with trans fats completely."

"So everyone should eat food that is low in sodium and low in fat to stay healthy," I said. "I guess more people should eat more of my mom's burritos! Both my mom and I want to show people that healthy food can taste delicious."

"That's fantastic, Carlos. So many people think that junk food is the only kind of food that tastes good. I'm glad to hear that you are going to show them otherwise!" said Dr. Chang.

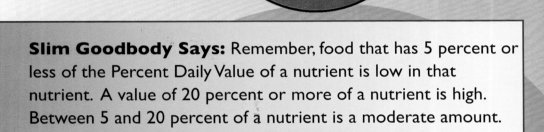

Slim Goodbody Says: Remember, food that has 5 percent or less of the Percent Daily Value of a nutrient is low in that nutrient. A value of 20 percent or more of a nutrient is high. Between 5 and 20 percent of a nutrient is a moderate amount.

Take a look at the Nutrition Facts label on Sal's macaroni and cheese on page 6 again. Would you consider the Percent Daily Value in one serving of macaroni and cheese to be high, moderate, or low in saturated fat? It is moderate, right? Since saturated fat is so unhealthy, even foods with a moderate amount of saturated fat are bad for you. Check out how you do on this little quiz:

1. Does this macaroni and cheese contain trans fats?
2. How about sodium? Is the Percent Daily Value of sodium high, moderate, or low?
3. Do you think the macaroni and cheese is a healthy choice?

(Answers 1. Yes 2. High 3. No)

PLENTY OF NUTRIENTS

Dr. Chang continued to run tests. "I have to admit it, Carlos. Your mother's burrito looks fantastic. Not only is it low in fat and sodium, it's high in all sorts of good nutrients. Most people don't eat enough healthy nutrients like dietary **fiber**, vitamin A, vitamin C, calcium, and iron in their diets. The whole-wheat tortilla and the beans are a great source of fiber. Foods that are high in fiber help your digestion and can reduce your risk of heart disease."

VITAMIN A
VITAMIN C
DIETARY FIBER
IRON

Slim Goodbody Says: Dry beans, fruits, and vegetables are other great sources of dietary fiber.

CALCIUM

"That's great!" I said with excitement. "Are there any other healthy nutrients in the burrito?"

"Well, the vegetables in the burrito are rich in vitamins. Orange vegetables, like the orange peppers in the salsa, have a lot of vitamin A. This nutrient helps keep your eyes and skin healthy. The cheese is rich in calcium, a mineral that helps build strong bones and muscles."

"So on the Nutrition Facts label, we can show that my mother's burritos are high in fiber, vitamins, and minerals?" I asked.

14

A VALUABLE TOOL

"You bet," answered Dr. Chang with a big smile. "The Nutrition Facts label helps people find food that has low amounts of unhealthy fats and sodium and high amounts of vitamins, minerals, and fiber. So you'll be able to show shoppers that your mother's burritos are a healthy choice. And if they taste as good as they smell, I think that you are going to have an easy time selling them!" she continued. "You still need to make sure that you get your Nutrition Facts label approved by the **Food and Drug Administration**. But it looks like you are well on your way to a thriving business, Carlos!"

"Cool! Thank you so much for your help," I said gratefully.

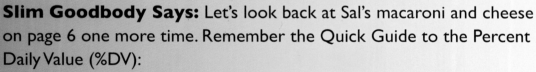

Slim Goodbody Says: Let's look back at Sal's macaroni and cheese on page 6 one more time. Remember the Quick Guide to the Percent Daily Value (%DV):

• 5 percent or less of the recommended daily value of a nutrient is LOW

• 20 percent or more of the recommended daily value of a nutrient is HIGH

1. Would you consider the Percent Daily Value in one serving of macaroni and cheese to be high or low in calcium?
2. What about the level of dietary fiber?
3. Do you think you should eat this macaroni and cheese if you were interested in increasing your intake of dietary fiber?

(Answers: High, 2. Low, 3. No)

THE LIST OF INGREDIENTS

When I got home from Dr. Chang's lab, I found my mother sitting at the kitchen table.

"Mom, I went to that food scientist, and I've got the information we need to make our own Nutrition Facts label!"

"Great!" My mom smiled. "I've been doing some work, too. Sal called with more information. We must follow the legal rules for food packaging. We'll need to include a list of the ingredients in our burritos on the package. We need to list the ingredients in order of their weight from the heaviest to the lightest."

"Geez, that sounds like a lot of work. Who looks at the ingredient list anyway?" I asked.

IMPORTANT INFORMATION

"Some people have **allergies** to certain foods like milk or peanuts. They have to read the ingredients list to make sure they don't eat something that will make them sick," my mother explained.

Slim Goodbody Says: Eight foods account for 90 percent of food allergy reactions: milk, eggs, peanuts, wheat, soy, fish, shellfish, and nuts from trees.

"That makes sense," I said.

My mother continued, "Other people use ingredient lists to make sure they're not eating unhealthy fats and added sugar."

Slim Goodbody Says: It's a good idea to steer clear of unhealthy or solid fats. If you see **hydrogenated** or partially hydrogenated oils in the ingredients list, try choosing a different food. It's also smart to limit foods with added sweeteners, such as corn syrup, high-fructose corn syrup, fruit-juice concentrate, maltose, dextrose, sucrose, honey, and maple syrup. These sweeteners are high in calories but don't give you the nutrients that you need to stay healthy.

"Yeah. Mr. Lawrence taught us that if an ingredient list starts with oils, fats, or sugars, it means that the food isn't healthy," I said. "He also said that you can usually tell if food is good for you just by looking at the length of the ingredient list. If the list is long and full of words that sound like chemicals, chances are that the food isn't healthy."

NUTRITION AND HEALTHY CHOICES

1. Nutrition Facts Label
2. Percent Daily Value
3. Calories /Empty Calories
4. Serving Size
5. Trans Fats
6. Saturated Fat

7. Dietary Fiber
8. Nutrients
9.

13. Ingredients lists

Slim Goodbody Says: Dimethylpolysiloxane and sodium acid pyrophosphate are examples of ingredients in food that sound like chemicals. In general, those ingredients are unhealthy. The more basic and straightforward an ingredients list is, the better.

Ingredients: pinto beans, mozzarella cheese (skim milk, thermophilic culture, and rennet), tortillas (whole-wheat flour, corn oil, water and salt), salsa (tomatoes, onions, orange peppers, vinegar, salt, and pepper), garlic, and salt.

"Well, we don't have to worry about that. My burritos are very simple and all natural," said my mother with confidence.

MAKING SURE THAT OUR MESSAGE IS TRUE

The next week, my mother and I were back in the kitchen, working on our packaging ideas.

"We need to think of ways to describe the burritos so that people will want to buy them. What if we print things like 'high fiber' and 'low fat' on the package?" I asked. "We want to send the message that our burritos are healthy."

"Well, the government has many rules about the kinds of words that you can use to describe your product," said my mother. She pulled out a printout from the U.S. Food and Drug Administration. This government department makes sure that our food and drugs are safe to use. We looked at the printout together.

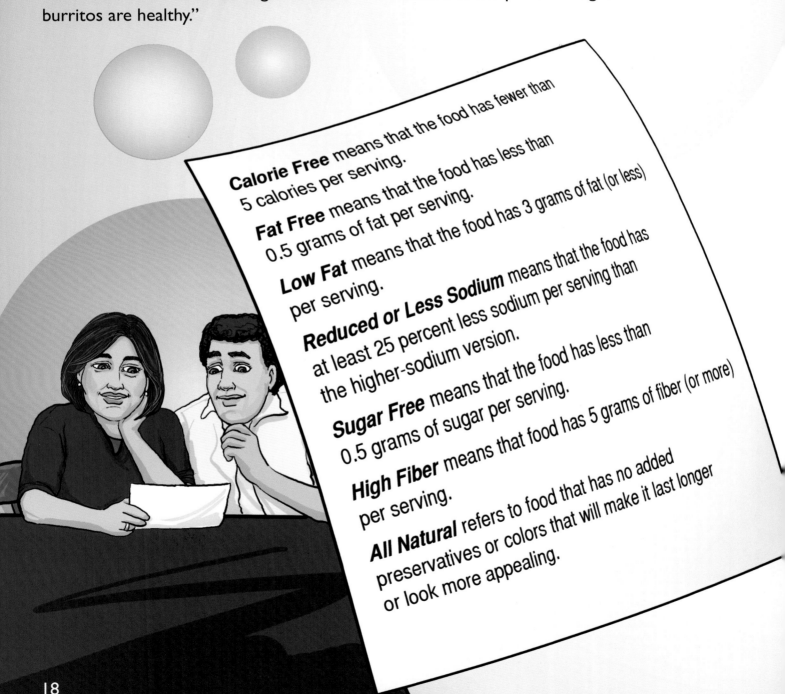

Calorie Free means that the food has fewer than 5 calories per serving.

Fat Free means that the food has less than 0.5 grams of fat per serving.

Low Fat means that the food has 3 grams of fat (or less) per serving.

Reduced or Less Sodium means that the food has at least 25 percent less sodium per serving than the higher-sodium version.

Sugar Free means that the food has less than 0.5 grams of sugar per serving.

High Fiber means that food has 5 grams of fiber (or more) per serving.

All Natural refers to food that has no added preservatives or colors that will make it last longer or look more appealing.

Slim Goodbody Says: Remember, low-fat food is not necessarily nutritious. Even a low-fat food can be high in sugar, which has many empty calories. For example, look at this list of ingredients for a low-fat caramel dip:

Corn syrup, sweetened condensed whole milk, high fructose corn syrup, water, butter (cream, salt), sugar, salt, disodium phosphate, artificial flavors (vanillin, ethyl vanillin), caramel color, pectin, potassium sorbate (preservative). CONTAINS: MILK

Remember, foods that begin with sugar or other sweeteners, oils, and fats in their ingredients list are often unhealthy. It's important to check the Nutrition Facts label and the ingredients list before eating something.

A HEALTHY NAME

"Well, from the looks of it, we can print 'High Fiber' and 'All Natural' on our package," I said. "We should also include something about how delicious the burritos taste."

"What about 'Benito's Burritos, Mouth-Watering Mexican Food. High in Fiber and All-Natural Ingredients!'?" suggested my mother.

"Perfect!" I said.

BEWARE OF OLD FOOD!

The next day, I was at my friend Johnny's house. We had been outside all afternoon, playing soccer in his backyard. When we got into the kitchen, Johnny threw open the refrigerator door and pulled out a gallon of milk. Then he went to the cupboard and took out a package of cookies.

"I'm starving," he said as he tore open the cookies.

"Cookies? Don't you have something healthier?" I asked.

A FOUL SURPRISE

"Come on, Carlos, we're not in health class," Johnny laughed.

"I know. But if I eat cookies right now, I'm going to feel awful in an hour. My body needs more than sugar after I've been running around," I explained. I poured myself a glass of milk. I took a huge gulp but then ran to the sink to spit it out.

"What's wrong?" Johnny asked, looking surprised.

I picked up the milk jug and looked at the date marked on the side. "See this date? This is the *sell by* date. November 15th! That was two weeks ago! This milk is sour," I said.

"Sell by date?" asked Johnny, looking confused.

"The grocery store is supposed to take food off of the shelf by this date. You can usually get away with keeping food for a few days after the sell-by date. Two weeks is stretching it though, dude".

WATCH FOR THESE DATES

"Now, if the date on the package is past its expiration date, you should throw the food away immediately," I explained. "There's also the best if used by date, which just means that the food tastes best if you eat it before that date passes."

"Geez, Carlos, you sound like a food encyclopedia!" said Johnny. "Where did you learn all of this?"

I laughed, "Now that my mom and I are starting our burrito business, I've had to learn about food safety laws. Did you know that grocery stores have to take baby food and formula off of the shelves once those products have passed their expiration dates? Other than that, food companies in most states don't have to print expiration dates on food. Many companies put them on to help customers make sure that their food is fresh, however. It's a good idea to keep an eye on dates, so you don't have to take a big sip of sour milk!"

Johnny laughed, "I guess you just learned your own lesson!"

Slim Goodbody Says: Now it's your turn. Take a look in your refrigerator at home. What kinds of foods have expiration dates, sell by dates, and best if used by dates? Can you find anything that has passed its expiration date? If so, it's time to throw it away!

MAKING DECISIONS, COMPARING PRODUCTS

While we were in the kitchen, Johnny's mother came home. "Johnny, can you run to the store for me?" she asked. "We're out of bread."

"Sure, Mom," said Johnny.

At the store, we found the bread aisle. Johnny sighed, "I never know what to buy. There are so many choices."

I told him, "My dad always tells me to use his decision-making tool when I'm buying food. First, you *identify your choices*. Then, you *evaluate each choice* and think about their consequences. Then, you *identify the healthiest decision* and *take action*. Afterward, it really helps to *evaluate your decision* to see if it was the right choice or not."

WHOLE-WHEAT VERSUS WHITE BREAD

Johnny picked up a loaf of whole-wheat bread and a loaf of white bread.

"It helps to read the ingredients list to evaluate your choices," I suggested.

He read aloud, "The whole-wheat bread is made from whole-wheat flour, water, wheat gluten, brown sugar, molasses, soybean oil, honey, yeast, salt, cultured wheat starch, oats, soy flour, and dough conditioners."

Johnny then looked at the other loaf. "The wheat bread is made with enriched wheat flour, water, high-fructose corn syrup, wheat bran, soybean oil, molasses, wheat gluten, salt, whey, calcium sulfate, and dough conditioners."

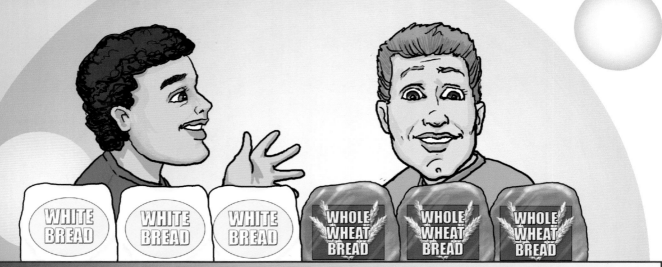

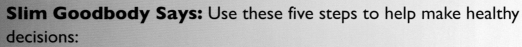

 Slim Goodbody Says: Use these five steps to help make healthy decisions:
- Identify your choices
- Evaluate each choice. What are the consequences of each choice?
- Identify the healthiest decision
- Take action
- Evaluate your decision

Johnny looked overwhelmed. "I don't know, Carlos. They sound pretty similar."

"One big difference is that the first loaf is made with whole-wheat flour. The second loaf is made with enriched wheat flour. Enriched wheat flour is just another name for white flour, and white flour isn't as healthy as whole-wheat flour," I explained.

Johnny began to evaluate his choices and their consequences. "OK. So the whole-wheat bread is more nutritious, and my family will be healthier if I buy it. I guess I'll choose that one."

"Now all you have to do is take action and buy it," I said. "And don't forget to evaluate your choice after you eat the wholewheat bread. Then, you'll know if you made the right decision," I said.

"Thanks, Carlos. You made my choice a lot easier," said Johnny.

Slim Goodbody Says: Now it's your turn. Look at these labels for two containers of milk. Remember to consider the serving size, the number of calories, and the amount of saturated fat and calcium in each before you choose the healthiest one.

REDUCED FAT MILK 2% Milkfat

Nutrition Facts
Serving Size 1 cup (236ml)
Servings Per Container 1

Amount Per Serving	
Calories 120	Calories from Fat 45

	% Daily Value*
Total Fat 5g	8%
Saturated Fat 3g	15%
Trans Fat 0g	
Cholesterol 20mg	7%
Sodium 120mg	5%
Total Carbohydrate 11g	4%
Dietary Fiber 0g	0%
Sugars 11g	
Protein 9g	17%

Vitamin A 10% •	Vitamin C 4%
Calcium 30% •	Iron 0% • Vitamin D 25%

*Percent Daily Values are based on a 2,000 calorie diet. Your daily values may be higher or lower depending on your calorie needs.

NONFAT MILK

Nutrition Facts
Serving Size 1 cup (236ml)
Servings Per Container 1

Amount Per Serving	
Calories 80	Calories from Fat 0

	% Daily Value*
Total Fat 0g	0%
Saturated Fat 0g	0%
Trans Fat 0g	
Cholesterol Less than 5mg	0%
Sodium 120mg	5%
Total Carbohydrate 11g	4%
Dietary Fiber 0g	0%
Sugars 11g	
Protein 9g	17%

Vitamin A 10% •	Vitamin C 4%
Calcium 30% •	Iron 0% • Vitamin D 25%

*Percent Daily Values are based on a 2,000 calorie diet. Your daily values may be higher or lower depending on your calorie needs.

The two kinds of milk have the same amount of calcium. The nonfat milk has no saturated fat, however, and has 40 fewer calories per serving than the reduced fat milk does. Did you choose the healthiest — the nonfat milk?

A Plan for Healthy Eating

A few weeks later, my mother and I went to the market with our first package of Benito's Burritos. We found Sal sitting in his usual spot behind the counter. I handed him the package.

He looked it over carefully. "You've got the Nutrition Facts label, the ingredient list, and a sell by date. Good work! Now for the real test," he said. We went to his back office, where he put the burrito in the microwave.

A few minutes later, the delicious smell of my mother's cooking filled the office.

"Incredible!" Sal said. "Come back with 30 more of these, and we'll be in business!"

"All right!" I said, hugging my mother. "Thanks, Sal!"

My Goals

When we got home, I said, "This has been such a cool project, Mom. Now that I've learned how important it is to eat healthy food, I want to try to eat less junk food."

"Why don't you set a goal to eat healthier food? It's easy," said Mom. "First, you *write down a realistic goal.* Then, you *list the steps that you will need to take to reach that goal.* Then, you *consider what kind of support you will need from your friends and family to reach* *your goal.* Then, you *evaluate your progress* and decide if you've been successful or not. And finally you can *reward yourself.*"

"All right, I guess there are a few steps that I can take to eat healthier. Most importantly, I can use the Nutrition Facts label and the ingredients list to choose food that is high in vitamins and fiber and low in saturated fat," I told her.

"Will you need any support from your friends and family?" asked my mother.

"If you and Dad buy healthy food at the grocery store, I won't be tempted to eat junk food at home," I said.

"I'd be happy to do that!" she smiled. "How will you reward yourself if you eat well for a couple of weeks?"

"Maybe if I eat well for a month, I'll buy myself a cool visor for my dirt bike helmet!" I said.

"That sounds fantastic, Carlos," said my mother.

Slim Goodbody Says: Now it's your turn! Use these five steps to set a goal for yourself:
- Set a realistic goal, and write it down
- List the steps to reach the goal
- Get help/support from others
- Evaluate your progress
- Reward yourself

BURRITOS FOR EVERYONE!

The school semester was ending. In health class, Mr. Lawrence asked us to prepare a final presentation of what we had learned about nutrition. For my presentation, I brought Benito's Burritos for every kid in my class.

I began my presentation by saying, "My mom and I started our own burrito business this fall. It's been a lot of work, but I've learned a lot about nutrition from it.

"Before selling our burritos at the store, we had to create a Nutrition Facts label. First, we had to figure out our serving size. Then, I brought the burritos to a food scientist, who

analyzed them. Dr. Chang helped us figure out the Percent Daily Value of the different nutrients in the burritos and the number of calories per serving.

"It was really cool. She ran all sorts of tests. Dr. Chang explained that our burritos were full of healthy nutrients like fiber, vitamin A, and calcium. She also said that they were low in the nutrients that you are supposed to avoid, like saturated fat and sodium."

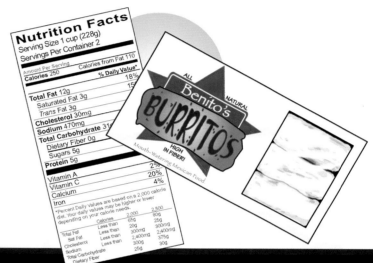

NUTRITION AND HEALTHY CHOICES

1. Nutrition Facts Label
2 Percent Daily Value
3. Calories/Empty Calories
4. Serving Size
5. Trans Fats
6. Saturated Fats

7. Dietary Fiber
8. Nutrients
9. Cholesterol
10. Expiration Date
11. Sell By Date
12. Best If Used By Date

13. Ingredient Lists

NUTRITION FACTS AND TRUTHFUL ADVERTISING

I continued, "After that, my mom and I designed the packaging for our burritos. We used the information from the food scientist to create a Nutrition Facts label. We wrote our ingredients list, too. We also wanted to print descriptions about the nutrients in the burritos, using words like 'All Natural' and 'Low-Fat' on the package. We had to find out if our burritos followed the government's rules about making these kinds of claims. We also added a sell by date to help customers know that our burritos are fresh. OK everyone, now you all get to try the burritos!"

"Awesome!" shouted Johnny. Soon my entire class was feasting on Benito's Burritos.

"These are incredible!" said Keisha. "I guess healthy food really can be delicious!"

"You bet. And there are plenty more where these came from at Sal's Market!" I shouted happily.

Slim Goodbody Says: What have you discovered about Nutrition Facts labels and ingredient lists from Carlos? Make a mind map of everything that you learned from this book to help you remember the important lessons about nutrition and choosing healthy food.

A New Role for Carlos

At the end of class, Mr. Lawrence came up to my desk. "That was a great presentation, Carlos. You did a fantastic job explaining what you learned about nutrition this fall, and your burritos are delicious," he said. "Congratulations on your new business!"

"Thanks, Mr. Lawrence. I couldn't have done it without your help. I came up with the idea for Benito's Burritos in your class, and your friend Dr. Chang, the food scientist, helped us a lot, too," I said gratefully.

"Carlos, have you ever considered becoming a health advocate?" asked Mr. Lawrence.

"What's that?" I asked.

An Agent for Healthy Change

"Health advocates are people who work to make their family, school, and community healthier and stronger. What you have to do is take a *healthy stand on an issue*. Then, you work to *persuade others to make a healthy choice*. And most importantly, you have to *be convincing*," explained Mr. Lawrence. "Is there a message you would like to spread?"

"Well, both my mom and I want to help people realize that healthy food can taste really good," I said. "I've thought about starting a nutrition club at school to spread that message. I'd like to help kids understand that eating well is important for staying healthy and growing strong. It seems like kids at our school only want to eat junk food. If we could show them how to read Nutrition Facts labels and ingredients lists, they might see how unhealthy their junk food is! I also think that our school should serve healthier food in the cafeteria. If I can get enough kids interested in eating healthy food, maybe we can persuade the school to serve healthy food that tastes good!"

"That sounds terrific, Carlos. You are going to be a great health advocate," said Mr. Lawrence. "Let me know when you start your nutrition club. I'd like to be a member too!"

Slim Goodbody Says: Now it's your turn to become a health advocate. Help your family, friends and community make healthier choices. Teach them how to read Nutrition Facts labels and ingredients lists. How will you persuade them to make healthy decisions? Remember, be convincing, and you will make your family and community stronger and healthier. Good luck!

Glossary

allergies Physical reactions, such as sneezing or watery eyes, to substances that do not make the average individual react the same way

calories Units of food energy; calories that are not burned through physical activity or everyday life are stored in the body as fat

carbohydrates The body's main energy source from foods. Most carbohydrates come from plants such as grains

cholesterol A fatty substance found in animal products. Meats, egg yolks, and dairy products, such as butter and cheese, contain cholesterol

consumers People who buy things

diabetes A disease in which people have too much sugar in their blood. People with diabetes cannot produce enough insulin, the substance the body needs to use sugar properly

fiber Material in food that cannot be digested but helps with going to the bathroom

Food and Drug Administration A government department that makes sure that food and drugs are safe to use

high blood pressure A condition that forces the heart to work harder to pump blood

hydrogenated Describes a liquid fat that has been chemically altered into a solid fat, such as butter or margarine

nutrients Chemical compounds (such as proteins, fats, carbohydrates, vitamins, or minerals) that make up foods. The body uses nutrients to function and grow

nutrition The study of food and diet

nutritious Describing foods that give the body energy and help it grow and heal

Percent Daily Value A section of the Nutrition Facts label that shows the amount of each nutrient in a serving of a food. It is usually based on a 2000-calorie diet

saturated fats Type of fats that usually come from animal products such as meat and dairy products. Saturated fats are solid at room temperature

sodium A mineral that is part of salt

trans fats Forms of fats found in solid fats, such as stick margarine, vegetable shortening, and some processed foods. Trans fats improve the flavor and texture of foods, but they increase the risk of heart disease

valid Based on facts or evidence

FOR MORE INFORMATION

Department of Health and Human Services

smallstep.gov/kids/flash/index.html

Learn more about food nutrition at this fun site for young people.

Family Education

life.familyeducation.com/nutrition/health/36613.html

Learn more about reading and interpreting Nutrition Facts labels.

Food and Drug Administration: Food Labeling and Nutrition

vm.cfsan.fda.gov/label.html

Learn more about Nutrition Facts labels and test your food label knowledge with a quiz! This site also offers a basic brochure on food labels.

Food and Drug Administration: Make Your Calories Count

www.cfsan.fda.gov/~ear/hwm/labelman.html

Download this interactive tool, and learn how to use the Nutrition Facts label to make healthy decisions about your diet.

INDEX

ABOUT THE AUTHOR

John Burstein (also known as Slim Goodbody) has been entertaining and educating children for over thirty years. His programs have been broadcast on CBS, PBS, Nickelodeon, USA, and Discovery. He has won numerous awards, including the Parent's Choice Award and the President's Council's Fitness Leader Award. Currently, Mr. Burstein tours the country with his live multimedia show "Bodyology." For more information, please visit slimgoodbody.com.